the

PAUL DANIELS

Magic

annual

CONTENTS

Published in Great Britain by
World International Publishing Limited.
A Pentos Company,
P. O. Box 111, Great Ducie Street, Manchester M60 3BL.
Printed in Belgium.
SBN 7235 6670 4.

HOW I BECAME A MAGICIAN

I was eleven years old when I first became interested in magic. I was on holiday in 1949 in Old Byland, near Helmsley, North Yorkshire, staying with a friend of my parents. It was a typical English summer with lots of rain. I was a very bored little boy until I saw a book, written in Queen Victoria's day, lying around the house. The title on the cover was *How to Entertain at Parties*, and looking through the pages I found a section 'How to Baffle Your Friends with Card Tricks'.

The pages that dealt with magic fascinated me. They were mostly self-working tricks but they were unlike anything I had ever read before.

Every page I turned absorbed me and it was then I decided there could only be one aim in my life: to be a magician.

The first trick I learned was easy enough to perform but it is a classic of its kind and I still perform it. What you have to do is prepare six cards as follows:-

1, 3, 5, 7, 9, 11, 13, 15, 17, 19, 21, 23, 25, 27, 29, 31, 33, 35, 37, 39, 41, 43, 45, 47, 49, 51, 53, 55, 57, 59, 61, 63

4, 5, 6, 7, 12, 13, 14, 15, 20, 21, 22, 23, 28, 29, 30, 31, 36, 37, 38, 39, 44, 45, 46, 47, 52, 53, 54, 55, 60, 61, 62, 63,

2, 3, 6, 7, 10, 11, 14, 15, 18, 19, 22, 23, 26, 27, 30, 31, 34, 35, 38, 39, 42, 43, 46, 47, 50, 51, 54, 55, 58, 59, 62, 63

8, 9, 10, 11, 12, 13, 14, 15, 24, 25, 26, 27, 28, 29, 30, 31, 40, 41, 42, 43, 44, 45, 46, 47, 56, 57, 58, 59, 60, 61, 62, 63

16, 17, 18, 19, 20, 21, 22, 23, 24, 25, 26, 27, 28, 29, 30, 31, 48, 49, 50, 51, 52, 53, 54, 55, 56, 57, 58, 59, 60, 61, 62, 63

32, 33, 34, 35, 36, 37, 38, 39, 40, 41, 42, 43, 44, 45, 46, 47, 48, 49, 50, 51, 52, 53, 54, 55, 56, 57, 58, 59, 60, 61, 62, 63

You will see that although the numbers on each *finish* with the same number (63) each of the six cards *starts* with a different number and none of the cards has the same set of numbers.

To perform this baffling Numbers Trick invite a member of your audience to think of any number between one and sixty-three. Let them look at the six cards and then hand you the cards on which their number appears.

YOU AT ONCE TELL THEM THE NUMBER OF WHICH THEY WERE THINKING!

The explanation is simple enough, *though you must never tell anyone.* Once you know the cards they have picked just add the top left hand number on each of these cards and you'll find they'll add up to the number selected.

Practise this before you perform and when you do, tell your audience this was the trick that started me off as a magician; maybe it will do the same for you.

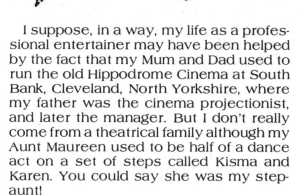

I suppose, in a way, my life as a professional entertainer may have been helped by the fact that my Mum and Dad used to run the old Hippodrome Cinema at South Bank, Cleveland, North Yorkshire, where my father was the cinema projectionist, and later the manager. But I don't really come from a theatrical family although my Aunt Maureen used to be half of a dance act on a set of steps called Kisma and Karen. You could say she was my stepaunt!

As a magician I am quite self-taught. I learned it all from books – and I still do. I didn't see a professional magician perform until I was twenty, and over the years I've managed to collect more than 5,000 books on magic was well as 8,000 magazines.

I still try out new tricks on Mum and Dad, and it's Dad who makes all the props I use in my act. He's a wonder worker with wood and metal.

That little Victorian party book that I found when I was an eleven year old schoolboy contained some intriguing card tricks so I got myself a pack of cards, followed the instructions and soon I was baffling not only my parents but anyone else who came along.

At fourteen I put on my first proper show – for the local Methodist Youth Club. I multiplied a few snooker balls and swallowed a few goldfish – or at least fooled the audience into thinking I had.

At sixteen I left school and went into a local government job as a junior clerk, from which I progressed to becoming an internal auditor – that's the chap who makes sure the ratepayers' money really *hasn't* vanished into thin air!

But, whenever I could, I kept myself busy practising conjuring tricks at home and then performing them at local concerts.

I was just eighteen when I was called up for National Service: a compulsory two years with the armed forces. The army sent me to Hong Kong and, of course, I took a few tricks with me so as to be able to entertain my chums with some magic.

I was serving with the Green Howards and I remember how I was driving a jeep one day near the border of communist China when I either mis-read the map or took a wrong turning and found myself in China itself.

Now China is famous for its magicians and one of the greatest tricks of all time is The Chinese Rings: the linking and unlinking of large metal rings.

At any moment I was expecting some real life Chinese rings to be slapped on me – as handcuffs! I was terrified some Chinese communist soldiers would find our little party and arrest us on the spot. Fortunately, no one noticed our mistaken 'invasion' and we were able to find our way back to British territory without being arrested.

While I was in Hong Kong I used to take part in Service concerts, and among the audiences I entertained were the crews of visiting US aircraft carriers.

By this time I had developed a quick, fast-moving act and this went down well with my American audiences – they appreciated speed.

Demobilized and back home I went back to local government and later went to work for my parents who were now running their own mobile grocery shop. I did a lot of shows at night and finished up doing so well that I saved enough money to buy my own shop.

But it was hard work and I was thrilled to get the offer of a full-time summer season at the Cosy Nook Theatre, Newquay; the same seaside resort where I was over the moon to be able to present my son Martin, now eighteen, in a summer show in 1981.

Magic, you see, really *does* now run in the Daniels family!

To return to my own early days: my debut as a full-time professional magician was in 1969. A year later Hughie Green put me into *Opportunity Knocks* and although I came second this TV debut led to more and more work both in England and abroad.

Johnny Hamp booked me for a spot in Granada's *Wheeltappers and Shunters* series and this is the television programme which really established me.

Johnny had created on television the atmosphere of a working men's club in the north of England, something with which I was more than familiar, for I had appeared in so many of them!

Just as all magicians must take care with the planning and presentation of their tricks, so I took extra care to make the most of my appearance on *Wheeltappers*.

I had noticed in the past that all these shows were taped in advance and many acts found their performances cut before they actually reached the screen.

Normally, a magician on TV does a few tricks and at a later stage, if the show is too long, it's an easy matter for the producer to cut or edit the performance.

I was determined that no part of my act would finish up on the cutting room floor,

so I devised a whole routine of borrowing a £5 note, vanishing it several times and finding it inside a walnut which had to be cracked open.

It lasted about twelve minutes and was presented in such a way that it was *impossible* for any TV technician to cut any part of it without spoiling the whole trick.

My catch phrase came to me quite spontaneously. I was working in a club in Bradford, Yorkshire, when a fellow heckled me and said something rude about the suit I was wearing.

I answered him by saying, "Oh, that's a shame because I like yours. Not a lot – but I like it."

This got a big laugh so I decided to keep it in the act.

I don't look upon myself as a great man of mystery. As far as my kind of magic is concerned, fun is what it's all about. This is not to say I don't enjoy mystifying you all, but my real aim is to entertain . . . to make you laugh . . . to keep you happy.

Not all of you can be a 'funjuror' (which is what I call myself) but if you can put a few good jokes into your tricks your audience will enjoy your performance all the more.

This is really how to succeed as a young magician. Be yourself. Find tricks and sayings that suit your own personality. Don't try to copy others. In the end, it's the performer who really matters. He's the one who entertains the audience – not the tricks.

Now that you're starting out to be a magician you'll teach yourself a lot of tricks. Maybe too many. But if you take my advice you'll stick to those which you are happiest performing – the ones that give *you* the most pleasure to perform, the ones that are the easiest for you but at the same time are the most effective.

Don't worry if a trick goes wrong, it happens to all of us sometime. You'll find, with experience, that you will learn to cover up your mistake and the chances are your audience will never spot the error.

For any beginner, it is best to first decide on the tricks you want to perform and then practise, practise, practise. It's not just a question of baffling your audience. You must develop your presentation so that you also entertain.

It worked for me when I was an eleven year old. I hope it will work for you.

FOR MY NEXT TRICK

I'm now going to tell you about some tricks that you will be able to perform at parties to amuse your friends. You'll find them easy enough to do but, remember, the art of the good conjuror is in the *presentation* of his art.

Don't try to perform any of these tricks without lots of rehearsal. All my tricks are carefully worked out beforehand and I always take great trouble to ensure they work smoothly before I show them to anyone. You must do the same.

* * *

Take a pack of 52 cards and announce that you are going to show your audience something very unusual about playing cards: "There are 52 cards in the pack," you announce. "And each pack has four suits containing 13 cards in each. The pack itself can be used to spell out exactly what these 13 cards are. Let me show you."

At this point you begin to deal the cards, face downwards, on to the table.

"A.C.E. spells ace," you tell them. "T.W.O. spells two. T.H.R.E.E. spells three."

You put down a card for every letter i.e., three cards for ace; three cards for 2; five cards for 3 and so on, right through the pack. The letters will actually spell all the cards in the pack:- ace, two, three, four, five, six, seven, eight, nine, ten, jack, queen, king.

The last four cards you put down will stand for K.I.N.G. and so the 52nd card will represent the letter G in the word king.

The explanation, of course, is that there are 52 letters if you spell the cards as I have shown – exactly the same number of cards as there are in the pack. Amazing, isn't it?

* * *

Get a friend to take a card from the pack. Tell him to put it behind his back so that you can't see it. While he does so, secretly look at the bottom card: let's` say it's the three of diamonds.

You then cut the pack into two halves. Your assistant has the choice of putting his card on top of either section.

If he puts his card on top of the pile with the three of diamonds, cut this section so that the bottom half is on top. This puts your three of diamonds immediately above the chosen card.

If he puts his card on top of the other pile all you have to do is place the section that has the three of diamonds on top again.

In other words, whatever pile he chooses you finish up with the three of diamonds *above* his card.

Invite your friend to cut the cards as many times as he likes. Then you deal the cards, holding them face down in your hand and turning them face upwards, one by one, on to the table.

When you come to the three of diamonds you know at once that the card that follows will be the chosen card.

Clever, isn't it?

* * *

"The harder I work the luckier I get."

11

You'll need a little sleight of hand for this one but it's not difficult providing you practise. First write down the name of any card you like on a piece of paper and seal this in an envelope. Put the same card on top of your pack of cards and you are all set. Invite a member of your audience to cut the pack of cards. When he has done so, place the envelope on top of one of the packs and get him to place the other portion on top again.

You thus have a pack of cards split in two sections by your envelope.

Tell your audience that you had a strange feeling beforehand that your friend was going to cut the pack at a certain card. Take off the top section of the pack and turn over the card at which he cut the pack. Hand him the envelope to open and inside he'll find that you have accurately predicted the same card.

To achieve this miracle, first place your sealed envelope on top of the pack and tell your friends it contains your prediction. When you lift the envelope and invite your assistant to cut the pack, just lift off the top card as well.

Keep the envelope and the hidden card in your hand while your friend cuts the pack and then casually put them back on top of one of the piles. Get him to put the other pile on top.

You now have the hidden card immediately beneath your envelope – half way through the pack. When the top section is removed your friends will be astonished to find the card beneath the envelope is the same as the one you named in your prediction.

Sneaky stuff!

* * *

Here's a good stunt for a party. You'll need a secret assistant, someone you can trust, for you have to arrange a simple code with him beforehand.

The idea is that you get your friends sitting round a table. *But you sit underneath.* Have one of them throw a dice and from underneath the table you're able to tell them the number that has come up on the face of the dice above you. The explanation is that your helper, unknown to everyone else, is signalling to you the number of spots on top of the dice.

To do this he places his hands on his knees under the table and signals to you; by the number of fingers he displays the exact number thrown.

Don't use thumbs – it may confuse you.

Real finger magic, don't you think?

* * *

Never despise the use of a secret confederate but never tell anyone that you are getting help in this way. Some of the greatest magicians in the world use secret assistants; there's no reason why you shouldn't do the same.

A secret assistant will also be needed for this next effect.

Have your audience select any object in the room during your absence. Return to the room, walk round the room slowly and then, without saying a word, you are able to announce the chosen object.

The explanation is simply that your unknown helper has tipped you off with a secret signal. Work out a sign between you beforehand.

He or she could scratch their nose when you face the object, adjust a tie or necklace. Any simple sign will do the trick for you.

If by chance you get the wrong object the first time, don't worry – just try again. This will merely impress your audience into thinking what a difficult feat you are trying to perform.

* * *

This is a card trick I first learned as a schoolboy. It's baffled everyone to whom I've shown it and there is no particular skill required to perform it other than the skill to present it in an attractive and entertaining manner.

Give your assistant two cards and invite him to place them in the pack, separately, anywhere he likes. Let's assume you have handed him the King of Clubs and Queen of Diamonds.

Don't draw attention to their suits, just call them 'the King and Queen'.

Once the two cards have been returned to the pack in their two different places, hold the pack firmly in your right hand and throw the cards on the floor – retaining the top card and the bottom card between your fingers.

This isn't at all difficult. Try it and see.

Now turn these two cards over and your audience will be amazed to find they are the King and Queen!

Hey, wait a moment, you'll say. How can that be? Well, the explanation is of course that they're *not*. It's just that the audience *think* they are.

Before starting the trick you prepared the pack by putting the Queen of Clubs and the King of Diamonds on the top and bottom. By the time you finish the trick the audience will only remember that one card was a club and the other a diamond. They won't recall which was which.

And it's *your* two Royal cards you flush out at the end – *not* the spectator's. In fact, you could call your feat a Royal Flush – *oooch!*

THE MAGIC CIRCLE

The world's most exclusive magical club is called the Magic Circle and it has been in existence for seventy-eight years.

I regard it as a great honour to be a member and to hold the club's highest magical degree, Member of the Inner Magic Circle (Gold Star). This degree is awarded by invitation only, which means that the President and Council of the Magic Circle invited me to join that elite band of one hundred and fifty members, worldwide, who are eligible to put the mystic initials of MIMC after their names.

The Magic Circle describes itself as 'the world's most exclusive club', the reason being that not every magician is able to become a full member.

First of all, anyone with a genuine interest in magic must be proposed and seconded by a Magic Circle member in order to become an Associate Member. Then, in order to progress further, one has to submit to a series of tests.

The first test, performed as an Associate Member, is to show some magical effects in our own clubroom before a judging panel of Magic Circle members. A further examination entitles the applicant to become an Associate of the Inner Magic Circle (Silver Star). From there, as I've already explained, he can proceed to Membership of the Inner Magic Circle – if his magic is good enough!

But we're a secretive lot. On joining, each member has to take a solemn oath not to disclose magical secrets to outsiders, so he can only discuss magical effects and how they are done with

fellow magicians.

The famous emblem of the Magic Circle is the signs of the Zodiac framed in a circle. Our Latin motto 'Indocilis Privata Loqui' means 'Not Apt to Disclose Secrets'.

You'll never get a member to tell you how a trick is done. Indeed, if he does so

you can be sure he is, in fact, trying to baffle you all over again with a false explanation.

One of the world's most famous illusions is 'Sawing a Woman in Half'. Nowadays it is possible to perform such a feat without the victim or even the volunteer assistant from the audience who

Andrew O'Connor

does the actual 'separating' having the slightest indication how such a magical miracle is actually performed.

We Circle members are proud of our ancient craft and you won't find us showing our audiences 'how things are done'. This doesn't mean, however, that we are not anxious to encourage new talent in our world of magic and this is why I have made a special point of telling you how to perform some simple tricks elsewhere in my first magic annual.

But the real secrets of magic will have to remain undisclosed until you are a fully fledged magician. Many of our mysteries are more than four thousand years old and have been handed down through generations of magicians from the days of the pharaohs.

Membership of the Magic

Johnny Hart with his 17 year old daughter on the stage of the MGM Grand at Reno, Nevada, USA, prior to vanishing this giant sports car in mid-air.

"The ball goes in the cup."

can't keep a secret. But, whatever the reason, our club doors remain locked to lady members. On the other hand, we now admit girl magicians to our Young Magician of the Year contest which is held every two years.

A number of young magicians who have won this coveted title have since become full time professionals and our most successful entrant was Johnny Hart who won the title when we first launched our contest in 1961.

Johnny, then an engineering student, became a full time international magician. Last year he was back starring in Las Vegas after appearing for a year at the MGM Grand in Reno.

And yet, if he hadn't entered for the Magic Circle contest none of this would probably have happened. I was happy to join him

"And now it's jumped from underneath to the top."

Circle is restricted to the male sex and you have to be eighteen years of age before you can join.

Our latest Young Magician of the Year. Andrew O'Connor, 18, who won the title in 1981, has now turned full-time professional. During the past year he has been touring with Hot Gossip, appearing in cabaret in Malta and enjoying a summer season at Torquay.

However, there are other magical societies accepting juniors and you'll find a list of these on page 48. Some of these, like the International Brotherhood of Magicians, also accept girl members.

So why does the Magic Circle bar its doors to lady magicians? Francis White, our President, likes to joke that it's because women

"You all saw it there."

myself as a Las Vegas star early last year.

We have several other young magicians who are working as full time professionals after winning this award, including Keith Cooper and Colin Rose.

In 1905 a group of magicians from the Midlands formed Britain's first magical society which they called, simply, the British Magical Society. Six months later, in the heyday of the Edwardian Music Hall, the Magic Circle was founded. All the great international performers of that time were members: Professor Hoffman; Will Goldston; P.T. Selbit; Servais le Roy; Maskelyne; Carl Hertz; Howard Thurston; Chung Ling Soo and David Devant himself, acknowledged Britain's greatest magician of this

century.

Many of their writings are still available at public libraries or from magical dealers. It would be well worth the while of any young aspiring magician to get hold of their books. The principles they describe are still in use today.

Our club was the brain child of Neil Weaver, an amateur magician, who arranged a meeting in a Soho restaurant to discuss the project. Twenty-three magicians attended and Weaver suggested the club should be called the Martin Chapender Club in honour of a young professional magician who had just died in the midst of a very successful career.

It was left to another professional magician, Louis Nikola, to put forward the suggestion that the club should not identify itself with any particular performer. He thought 'The Magic Circle' would be a much better title.

Weaver stood his ground until someone remarked that Martin Chapender's initials were M.C., the same as those for Magic Circle.

A vote was taken and it was agreed to adopt the title 'The Magic Circle'.

David Devant was our first President and the first edition of our monthly magazine *The Magic Circular* appeared in 1906 edited by Nevil Maskelyne, son of the original John Nevil Maskelyne who, partnered by Devant, presented a regular magic show with two performances daily.

These were staged in their own theatre, St. George's Hall, close to Broadcasting House, the BBC's HQ in Portland Place, London, and now the site of St. George's Hotel. Maskelyne and Devant's magical presentations ran for nearly thirty years. Before Devant joined him, Maskelyne ran his 'House of Mystery' at the Egyptian Hall, Piccadilly.

The Magic Circle's first permanent home was Anderton's Hotel in Fleet Street, heart of the newspaper world. Regular Monday night meetings were held there for twenty-five years until our membership had grown so large we had to find larger premises.

Several more moves

were made and it wasn't until 1968 that we settled in our present HQ just off Tottenham Court Road. We have our own theatre, museum, club room and, of course, our library, which contains one of the most complete records of magical history in the world.

Here, any of our 1,400 members can browse among the 1,000 plus volumes that form our lending and reference libraries. Every magical secret is in their covers; we even have a 1584 copy of Reginald Scot's famous *Discoveries of Witchcraft,* the oldest book on magic still in existence.

Behind glass fronted cabinets there are shelves of old time conjuring tricks and apparatus on display, each of them a collector's item.

No other similar society in the world can boast of such a fine club room with such amenities; the only snag on the horizon, as I write, is that we have been given notice to quit owing to the expiration of our lease, with the result that a search is now going on to find new premises.

But, wherever these may be, we will continue with our policy of having club meetings every Monday evening when special

events are staged: lectures on the magical art not only by our own members but also by visiting magicians from the USA and other parts of the world; competitions; quizzes; demonstrations by magical dealers and similar functions of interest to our members.

Such functions are, of course, confined to members and their guests. Many are closed events which means that guests can only be admitted by special permission.

During the year we do stage a number of events which are open to the general public; our annual week-long show is world famous and there are other regular fixtures including our club room 'At Homes' to which the public are admitted.

If you would like to have

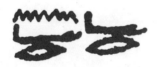

details of such gatherings just send a stamped addressed envelope to Mac Wilson, MIMC, Deputy Secretary, 29 Shepperton Road, Petts Wood, Kent.

As in our early days, our members include all the world's top professional magicians.

Our most distinguished member is Prince Charles, who visited us in October 1975. After watching a number of magicians perform he indicated that he had always been interested in magic and would very much like to become a member.

Francis White, our President, told the Prince that the Circle would be pleased to invite him to become a member of the Inner Magic Circle, but as he was skipping the previous degrees which lead up to this invitation he would have to perform some magical feat to justify his admittance to such an elite corps of conjurors.

The Prince was well prepared for this. In fact, he had been coached in advance by Robert de Pas, one of our members, a Lieutenant Commander in the Royal Navy who had been a Flag

Egyptians performing the classic "Cup and Ball" trick as painted on the wall of a burial chamber in Ben Hassan in 2500BC.

Lieutenant to the late Earl Mountbatten, the Prince's uncle.

Prince Charles then set about performing the classic Cups and Balls routine, the world's oldest know sleight of hand trick. There is a drawing of it being performed on the wall of an ancient Egyptian burial chamber in Beni Hassan. And the date? 2,500 BC. It is still a favourite among magicians.

Hieronymous Bosch, the Flemish artist, left a famous painting of the same trick dating back to the 15th century. It hangs in the municipal museum of Saint-Germain-en-Laye, France.

The Cups and Balls is usually performed as a close-up effect although, personally, I have always managed to hold an audience's attention by also presenting it on the stage or in cabaret. Prince Charles did the same.

For there are many forms of magic: close-up effects, performed to a small group around a table require quite different techniques to major illusions.

A close-up magician usually performs in a quiet, intimate sytle, while illusion magic requires a more flamboyant presentation; a whole stage and a larger audience.

Then there is the Tommy Cooper style comedy magic where everything appears to go wrong; magical dexterity with cards, thimbles, doves and similar objects for sleight of hand effects with the performer usually not saying a word; paper folding tricks (or origami, as originated by the Japanese); Punch and Judy (forerunner of the Muppets) and many more.

The Magic Circle has members who are expert in all these fields.

I am proud to be one of them.

The Conjurer by Heironymus Bosch.

20

FUN WITH FIGURES

In this section I'm going to give you some tricks that you can do with figures. You'll be able to challenge your friends with them and all you'll need is some paper and pencils.

First, here's a little contest with which you will be able to catch your friends.

Put down these figures: 7,777 and ask your friend to read them. He'll say they total seven thousand, seven hundred and seventy seven. Quite correct.

Now ask him to write down eleven thousand, eleven hundred and eleven. Most people, unless they know the secret, will get it wrong.

For the correct answer is 12,111. Try this out and see how many get it right. I don't think there will be many.

* * *

Tell your friend to think of a number but you must not be told what it is. Let's agree, as an example, the number is 5. Then tell him to carry out the following but not to tell you the results.

Multiply the number by itself. He will then have 25.

Next he must take 1 from the first number he thought of. Result: 4. This must also be multiplied by itself, making 16.

He subtracts this sum (16) from his first total (25) and the result is 9.

Now tell him to add 1 to this total and this will give him 10. Ask him to tell you this final number, halve it and you can at once tell him his original number: 5.

You'll find this will work every time but as I never believe you should ever do the same trick in the same way twice I am going to give you a different method of performing this great numbers trick.

This time get your friend to multiply the number he first thought of by 3. Let's assume he again thought of 5. So this gives you 15. Tell him to add 1 and this gives you 16. Instruct him to multiply this number by 3 and add the first number he thought of. The result will be 48 plus 5 which equals 53.

As it happens, the result must always end with 3 and this makes it easy for you to tell him the original number: it's always the other digit, in this case 5.

* * *

"Being happy in your work is probably the most important thing because too much of your life revolves around it."

Here's a way you can use figures to discover the hidden word in a book. Have your friend look at a book with fewer than 100 pages and tell him to open it at any page he chooses.

Then get him to select any word on any of the first 9 lines of that particular page. The word must also be among the first 9 words on that particular line.

Make sure he doesn't tell you the page, the line or the word he has chosen. Then tell him you will discover the word by using mathematical magic.

For example, let's suppose he has opened the book at page 63, chosen the fifth line and then the seventh word which happens to be cocoa. This is what you have to do:

1. Ask him to double the number of the page	126
2. Multiply the answer by 5	630
3. Add 20 to the amount	650
4. Add the number of the line (5)	655
5. Add another 5	660
6. Multiply this total by 10	6600
7. Add the number of the word (7th)	6607
8. Subtract 250 in any case	6357

Get him to tell you the total, which will be 6357. This at once tells you the page is 63, the line is number 5 and the word is number 7.

Pick up the book, turn to page 63, count down to the fifth line and select the seventh word.

All you have to do is to call out the word – cocoa.

Use a pocket calculator if you have one.

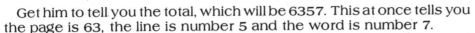

* * *

Here's something else you can try. It's a puzzle, but all the clues are given with the question.

If John was a year older he would now be the same age as Bill was this time last year.

If he was a year younger, he would only be half as old as Bill will be this time next year.

How old are John and Bill?

See if you can work this out for yourself. I have put the answer on page 20.

* * *

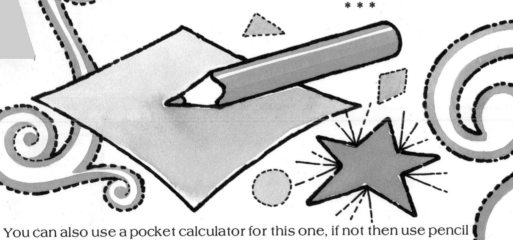

You can also use a pocket calculator for this one, if not then use pencil and paper.

Ask your friend if the house or flat where he lives has a number and also if he is willing to tell you the truth about his age. If he answers 'yes' to both questions then get him to carry out your instructions. But he mustn't tell you the result until you have finished.

First he writes down the number of his home. Then he doubles it and adds 5. Next he multiplies by 50 and adds his age. Now he must add the number of days in a year (365). Finally, he subtracts the original number of MPs in the House of Commons (615).

Ask him the result and you can then tell him not only the number on his front door but also his age.

This is because the first two figures of the final sum will be the number of your friend's home and the second will be his age.

If it should happen that your friend's front door is numbered below 10 then it will be the first figure only that indicates the number. If the house number is in three figures then the final total will consist of five figures and the first three numbers will be on his front door.

If it's a leap year, 366 will have to be added. To allow for this, tell your friend to add 4 instead of 5 when you give him your third instruction.

* * *

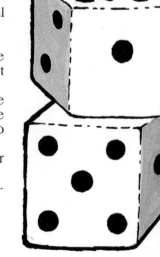

Have your friend think of three figures. Invite him to double any one of them. Then he must multiply the answer by 5 and add either of the two numbers of which he is thinking.

Next he has to multiply the answer by 10 and add the last remaining number. The final answer will consist of the three numbers which he first selected in his thoughts!

To show you how this works, let's suppose his three figures were 7, 1 and 4:

Double the 7	... 14
Multiply by 5	... 70
Add in the 1	... 71
Multiply by 10	... 710
Add in the 4	... 714

To present this as a trick get your friend to write the three original numbers on a piece of paper and seal it in an envelope.

This envelope remains sealed throughout the trick.

At the end of his addition and multiplication ask him to pass you the piece of paper on which he has been making his calculations. Glance at it casually and then proceed to tear up the paper.

One quick look will have given you the total and if you tear up the paper as soon as you have this information the chances are that he won't remember that this final total has provided you with the clue to his original figures.

After tearing up the paper, take your time. Announce each number separately as though it's a great mental effort.

Then, when the sealed envelope is opened your friend will be suitably astonished.

* * *

Here's a quickie for you. I can't promise it will work every time but the odds are in your favour that you will be successful.

I *can* promise you that if it works it will be completely baffling.

Get someone to select a number between 1 and 10. Generally the number chosen will be 7. Invite someone else to pick a number between 1 and 5 and you'll find that 3 is usually chosen.

Have both these numbers written on a piece of paper beforehand with the words 'I PREDICT YOU WILL CHOOSE THE NUMBER 7' or 'I PREDICT YOU WILL CHOOSE THE NUMBER 3'.

Don't worry if they don't select either a 7 or a 3, just say, "So that's your lucky number. I just wanted to know," and proceed with another trick.

* * *

This is a very clever trick if you're good at simple maths but if you can't add up quickly you'd better leave it alone, unless you can use a pocket calculator for the addition.

The effect is to predict the result of a sum, when added up, from numbers having been called out at random by members of the audience.

You'll need a pad and pencil handy but first put your prediction in a sealed envelope and, for the benefit of this illustration, we'll decide on the number 23,843.

This is the total at which you are going to arrive at the end of your demonstration and this is the number you put into the sealed envelope.

Here's how you reach this result:

Remove the first digit (2) from the number and add it to the grand total. Your audience will now see you write on your pad

3,845

Have one of your audience write down a four digit number beneath. They have complete freedom of choice, e.g.

3,845

1,528

Below this, you write another four digit number. Give the impression your number has been selected quite haphazardly but, in fact, you put down under each digit of the spectator's number the number required to make a total of 9.

Your paper should now look like this:

3,845

1,528

8,471

Get another member of the audience to put down a row of four figures below yours, any figures he wishes. Then you write a fifth number to finish things off, again choosing digits that will add to 9.

Your final sum will now look like this:

3,845	your first number	
1,528	your assistant's number	} the columns of these two
8,471	your second number	lines total 9,999
2,911	your assistant's number	} the columns of these two
7,088	your final number	lines total 9,999
23,843	FINAL TOTAL AS PREDICTED	

In this example the first digit of the number you predicted is 2. This means your audience must add two lines and you must add another two lines, making five lines to be added together at the close.

If you pick a predicted number with 3 as the first digit, then there have to be three pairs of lines adding up to 9; if 4 then it has to be four pairs and so on.

Always remove the first digit of the predicted number and add it to the number that remains and, remember, you must always add the same number of digits every time.

* * *

Here's another prediction trick which is very easy to do. Invite a friend to write down the year he was born and add to this the date of some important event in his life.

To this sum he adds his age (up to December 31st of the current year) and finally the number of years since that important event he selected actually happened.

Now you'll have had no difficulty at all in knowing this total beforehand and to have made your prediction in the classic manner: in a sealed envelope.

How come? Well, the total of these four numbers will always be twice the current year.

How's that for a neat trick?

* * *

Now for a little puzzle which has mystified many audiences.

The performer turns his back and invites a member of his audience to take some matches out of a matchbox and form them into three small heaps.

He can use any number of matches he likes but he has to count out the heaps and ensure that the number of matches in each heap are the same; and there must be more than three matches in each pile.

Someone else in the audience is then invited to select any number between 1 and 12.

Our young wizard is now able to give directions for moving the matches around so that the number in the middle heap finishes up the same as the number selected.

To achieve this, have the spectator take three matches from each of the two end heaps and place them on the centre pile. Then the spectator is asked to count the number in one of the end piles and remove that number from the centre pile. He can choose either heap. Again, he places these matches at whichever end he likes.

The effect of this is always to leave nine matches in the centre pile. Then it's an easy matter for you to give the appropriate instructions to add or subtract the right number of matches so that this centre pile will total the requested number between 1 and 12.

Get the (match) point?

* * *

This is an ingenious coin trick for any young magician to perform and like many good tricks it's very simple.

Have someone place a handful of loose change on the table. Turn your back and suggest somebody starts turning the coins over, one by one. They can pick the coins at random and even turn the same coin over as many times as they like.

But, each time he turns over a coin he has to call out 'TURN'.

Your assistant can continue with this procedure as long as he likes. Finally, he has to cover one coin with his hand. You turn around and at once tell him whether the coin under his hand is heads or tails.

To achieve this minor miracle just count the number of heads showing on the coins before you turn your back. Every time your friend calls out 'TURN' you add 1 to this number.

You will now have the final total which you must remember when you turn around to face your audience.

"How's this for a cute bunny?"

If the total is even, there has to be an even number of heads on the table (including the covered coin). If the total is odd, then the number of heads will be odd (including the covered coin).

On turning round, a glance will tell you whether the covered coin is heads or tails, i.e., if you have an even number and the heads are even, then the hidden coin will be tails. If you have an odd number and the heads are even, then the hidden coin has to be heads. Similarly, if you have an even number and the heads are odd then the hidden coin must be heads and if you have an odd number and the coins are odd, then the hidden coin will be tails.

In short, the covered coin will be heads or tails depending on whether a head is needed to make the total even or odd.

I suggest you follow these instructions a few times to understand how it all works and then practise seriously.

It's a real *coin*cidence!

* * *

Meet **Ali Bongo**

Ali Bongo has been my friend, magical adviser and behind-the-scenes helper since my early days on BBC TV. Until I met him I had no idea how much we have in common.

How about this for coincidence?

We both learned about magic from books.
We both started as boy magicians.
We both spent two years in the army.
We were both on Hughie Green's talent show 'Opportunity Knocks'.
We both work for laughs.

Ali is also a fellow member of the Inner Magic Circle and a very knowledgeable chap when it comes to working out new mysteries for my TV shows.

You see him many times on television – a zany-looking character with a long droopy moustache and odd oriental headgear. That's when he's doing his famous Ali Bongo act – the Shriek of Araby – which has had audiences laughing throughout the world.

At other times he pops up as a 17th century footman, in white wig, glasses and knee breeches.

Ali is acknowledged a great expert on all things magical and you will see he is credited as Programme Associate on the list of credits which appear on the TV screen after my BBC TV programmes.

I am very happy and proud that he is associated with me and I'm delighted to be able to tell you more about him.

He took his funny-sounding name after playing the part of a character called Ali Bongo in a village hall pantomime as a teenager.

He was supposed to be a mad-cap Eastern chef aboard a ship; he didn't have to do any magic, but his antics on the stage brought so much laughter from his audience that he decided to develop the character as a comedy conjuror.

Ali had actually done his first trick when he was five years old (we magicians start young)! He was then living in India where his father was an Indian Army officer.

His interest in magic came at first from books. Back in England, as a schoolboy, he started 'The Crimson Circle Conjuring Club' with a magazine which he wrote and illustrated himself while a student at Sutton Valence School in Kent.

At seventeen, he was working with a firm marketing duplicators and earning extra money as a children's entertainer in Kent in his spare time. A year later he founded the Medway Magical Society which is still going strong today.

Throughout his National Service with the Royal Army Pay Corps he spent all his spare time doing tricks, inventing tricks and writing about tricks for magical magazines.

Originally, Ali used to talk to his audiences while performing but, early in his career, decided to change his style and become a silent magician which he has stuck to ever since.

You have to be a very good magician indeed to succeed without speaking and to get laughs as well takes even more skill.

Ali has become a master of silent comedy. His technique is based on the old silent films where comedians like Charlie Chaplin were able to entertain with mime, funny faces and extravagant movements.

He is a perfectionist and will take weeks to develop a new trick or a new routine before showing it to the public. He maintains that 'nothing is ever so perfect that it cannot be improved'.

Like all we magicians he keeps his secrets. And not only his magical ones.

If you'd like him for your party look him up in the London phone book and he's Ali Bongo; talk to his mother and she'll tell you she's Mrs. Bongo.

For that's his most guarded secret of all – his real name.

After National Service he joined a magic dealer as a demonstrator and salesman. He also made up tricks, packed them, wrote the instruction sheets and did the illustrations. For Ali is also an accomplished artist and has illustrated not only magic books but also contributed cartoons and humorous drawings to newspapers and magazines.

From his first job Ali progressed to becoming manager of the magic department of the famous Hamleys Toy Shop in Regent Street, London. Thanks to him lots of youngsters became interested in magic.

All the time he continued working in his spare moments as a magician and after four years he became a full time professional.

Since then, his crazy Arabian Nights outfit and his zany tricks have been seen in America, Japan, Germany, France, Switzerland and many more countries.

He's a regular performer on the BBC's *Crackerjack* and although, unlike me, he never says a word, he is able to entertain in a truly magical manner.

HEADS I WIN, TAILS YOU LOSE

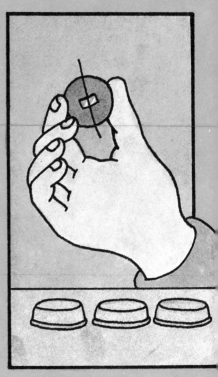

Now for some Heads I Win, Tails You Lose tricks. These are some of the 'You Can't Win' stunts I have been putting over on TV as a fairground barker in my Bunco Booth sequence.

For a start, take one of those flat book matches, show it to your assistant and then put three crosses on one side with a pencil.

Tell him you will throw it in the air and if it comes down with the crosses uppermost you will give him £1. But, more than that, tell him if it comes down on the *other* side, i.e., the side *without* the crosses, you will still give him £1.

Throw it in the air – and it comes down on its edge. How to do it? Just bend the match before you throw it upwards.

Paul with Spanish superstar Julio Iglesias after interviewing him on his BBC radio series.

You'll need a coin and three metal bottle caps large enough for the coin to fit underneath.

Tell your assistant that no matter how he places the metal caps you'll always be able to say where the coin is.

Challenge him to do the same.

For a start, place the coin under one of the caps and move them around very quickly. The likelihood is that your assistant will have lost sight of the coin but you can at once tell him where it is.

The explanation is that you have switched the coin for another when he wasn't looking. And the coin you use for the trick has a strand of hair stuck underneath with a small piece of sticky tape.

From then on, you can see at a glance under which cap the coin is hidden.

If you don't feel capable of switching the coins, start with the prepared coin on the table with the hair facing you. There's no need for it to be picked up. Just place one of the bottle caps over it; switch the caps around and you'll still be able to tell where the coin is.

This trick works best if performed on a tablecloth with a broken pattern – you can see the hair easily enough because you are looking for it.

* * *

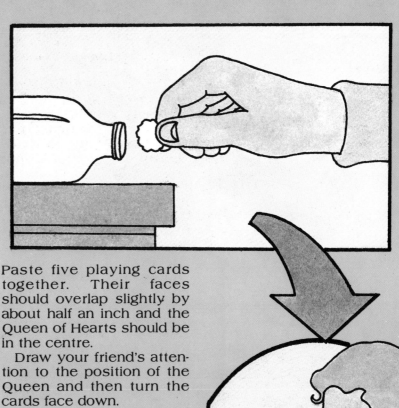

Paste five playing cards together. Their faces should overlap slightly by about half an inch and the Queen of Hearts should be in the centre.

Draw your friend's attention to the position of the Queen and then turn the cards face down.

The challenge is for your friend to put a paper clip on the Queen of Hearts.

After his attempt, turn the cards over to show their faces and you'll find that the paper clip is nowhere near the Queen of Hearts.

Don't ask me why this always happens – but it does.

* * *

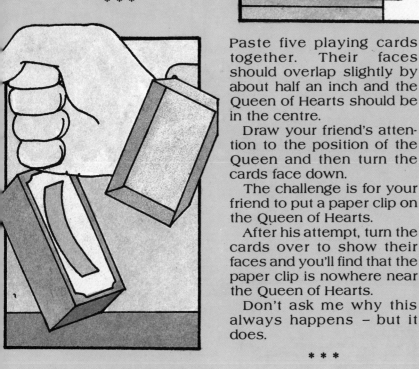

Get hold of an empty matchbox, the wooden variety.

Stand the cover on a table and balance the drawer on top.

Now challenge your friend to crush the matchbox by bringing his fist down on the top of the drawer with a sharp blow.

No matter how often he tries he'll find it quite impossible to achieve this; as soon as his fist strikes the drawer both sections of the matchbox will fly smartly away from the descending blow.

* * *

Place an empty milk bottle on its side on the edge of a table. Now roll up a piece of paper, about the size of your finger nail and put it resting in the neck of the bottle.

Ask your friend to blow it right inside. It can't be done unless you know how. If you blow directly at the small ball of paper it will just keep flying out in your face. The only way to ensure it enters the rest of the bottle is by using a drinking straw and blowing directly at the ball of paper.

* * *

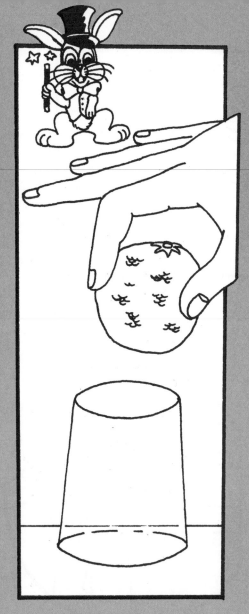

Take a piece of paper, half the size of a page in this book will do nicely, and with a pair of scissors make one cut from the bottom to about half way to the top, say about two or three inches from the right edge. Then make another cut about three inches further on.

You now have a piece of paper with two cuts going upwards from the bottom edge making three sections. The top edge remains intact.

Make sure each segment is the same size and then challenge someone in your audience to pull the two side pieces so that he tears the paper into three.

However he pulls he will always fail. The paper will always tear into two pieces, not three.

* * *

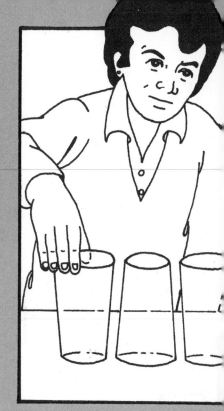

Line up three tumblers with the outside two the right way up and the middle one upside down.

Now, in three moves, turning two glasses at a time, you proceed to turn all the glasses upside down.

Invite someone from your audience to do the same but they will fail unless they know the secret.

And here it is: let's imagine the glasses are numbered from left to right 1-2-3.

The first turn is glasses 2 and 3.

The second turn is glasses 1 and 3.

The final turn is glasses 2 and 3 again.

Each of the three glasses will now be upside down.

Now, with confidence, turn the *middle* one the right way up and invite someone else to try it.

They rarely spot that the 'set up' is now the opposite to the way you started.

I performed this 'con trick' in the Bunco Booth in my BBC TV series.

* * *

Place a tumbler upside down on your table.

Invite your assistant to place an orange, coin or other small object on top of the glass.

Tell him you'll give him £1 if he gets it right.

Naturally, he places the object on the top of the upturned glass and reaches for the £1 he has won.

But don't let him get it.

"Oh no," you say, "I said on the top of the glass and you've put it on the bottom."

* * *

34

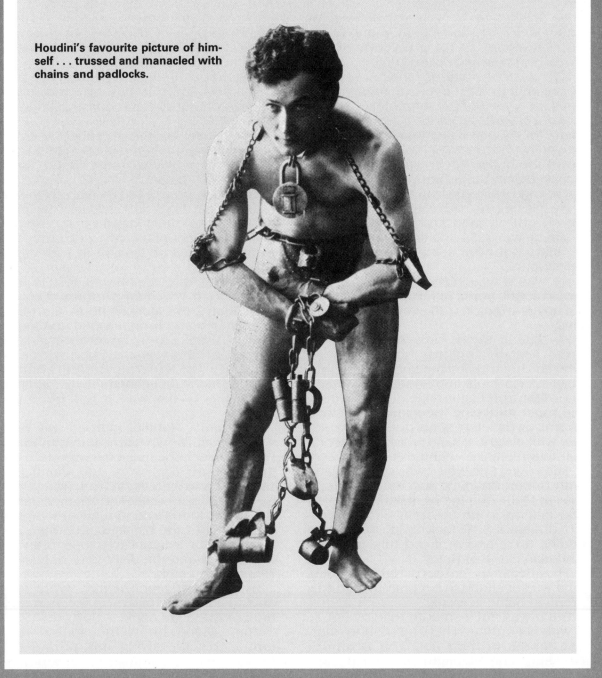

Houdini's favourite picture of himself . . . trussed and manacled with
chains and padlocks.

THE MAGIC OF HOUDINI

Houdini is the most famous name in the history of magic and no book dealing with the oldest of the theatrical arts would be complete without a tribute to this great magician.

Houdini's interest in magic started, like most of us, when he was very young – just 14. We even have the same birthday – April 6th! – though Houdini was born in 1874, in Budapest, Hungary. His real name was Erich Weisz which became Eric Weiss when his parents emigrated, first to England and then to Appleton, Wisconsin, USA.

His father was a poor Jewish rabbi. At eight years old Eric Weiss was selling newspapers and working as a shoe-black. At 12 he ran away from home in search of regular employment so that he could send money back to his impoverished parents.

He finished up in New York where his father joined him and together they saved enough money to bring his mother and three brothers from Wisconsin.

Life was very tough for the future magical headliner but, even in those early days, he was most resourceful. Aged 14, and out of work, he joined a group of applicants for a job at a tie making firm. Undismayed by the length of the queue he took down the notice advertising the job, told the assembled applicants it was no longer vacant and walked in to get the job himself.

By this time he had begun to read books on sleight of hand and during the two years he worked at the tie manufacturer's he started to give shows to friends and neighbours.

He was also a keep-fit enthusiast and would spend hours at the local gym building up his strength with exercises and jogging.

His idol in these early days was the great French conjuror Robert-Houdin, who has been called the father of modern magic. A clockmaker by trade, he brought his skill as a precision engineer to devising the most intriguing mechanical illusions as well as developing his personal expertise with sleight of hand which the French call 'legerdemain' – lightness of the hand.

The young Eric Weiss was so enthralled with Robert-Houdin's success in Europe that, at 17, he quit the tie making business and embarked on a career as a professional magician. He took his idol's name by adding an 'i' and prefixed this with the Christian name of Harry.

Thus began the career of Harry Houdini, who was destined to become the world's greatest name in magic.

But it was not a smooth road.

With his brother Theo, he tried to interest agents in their act 'The Brothers Houdini'. The highlight of their performance was 'Metamorphosis' (or 'Change of Form').

This illusion is still around today. You've probably seen it on the stage or on TV.

The magician's assistant is manacled and placed inside a sack. The top of the sack is tied and the sack is then placed inside a large wooden box. This box is padlocked and roped.

The magician stands on top of the box and lifts a hooped covering around himself, completely hiding the magician and the box beneath. All you can see is the magician's hands holding the top edge of the circular frame.

In a flash the frame is lowered and there stands the magician's assistant, free of his manacles, the locked box and the sack in which he was imprisoned.

The box itself remains securely tied and padlocked and it is now the turn of the assistant to unlock the box and undo the ropes.

Inside the box the audience sees the same sack but when it is opened it is the turn of the magician to be found, manacled, inside the sack.

This trick, performed by Houdini in 1891, is as baffling today as it was then. Siegfried and Roy, acknowledged as the world's greatest illusionists, are currently performing the same illusion in Las Vegas, U.S.A.

However, this illusion was not a Houdini invention. It was first performed by our own John Nevil Maskelyne as a straightforward escape from a roped and locked box in 1865. Later, several magicians, including Robert-Houdin, improved on the idea but it was left to the Brothers Houdini to bring in the fast-change twist. And ever since this is the way it has been presented.

At twenty, Houdini married. His bride was a small, brown-haired girl from Brooklyn and, since the magician was also of no great stature, they were a good match on the stage and were soon working together as 'Professor Houdini and his assistant'.

They included a mind-reading routine in their act, but the highlight was their presentation of Houdini's escape from the locked box and the discovery of his wife Bess in his place.

By constant practice they were soon able to exchange places in the incredible time of three seconds.

They played variety; they toured with a circus. It was during this period that Houdini began his interest in lock picking, ecaping from chains and handcuffs and, on one occasion, he freed himself from a strait-jacket (a device used to restrain violent prison inmates).

In addition to working as a husband and wife magic act, Houdini began taking an interest in the spiritualist mediums of his day, people who claimed it was possible to communicate with the dead through their own special powers.

Houdini considered all such claims were fraudulent and set about exposing the mediums by duplicating everything they did.

He put scores of them out of business and became an arch enemy of the whole spiritualist movement.

But it was as an escape artist that he first began hitting the headlines. Wherever he went he never lost the opportunity to work out a special escape stunt from the local jail so as to attract people to his performance in the theatre.

He would challenge the police to strip him of all his clothes, manacle and lock him in one of their cells. Yet he would still escape.

He billed himself as 'The Undisputed King of Handcuffs', 'Monarch of Leg Shackles' and 'Champion Jail Breaker'.

It was in England that the 26-year-old Houdini achieved his greatest success and it was our own Scotland Yard that set him on the path to the revered position his name still holds, nearly sixty years after his death.

He had come to London in 1900 with a book of press cuttings, seeking an engagement at the old Alhambra Music Hall in Leicester Square (now the Odeon Cinema).

But the theatre manager, for whom Houdini auditioned, wasn't all that impressed though he liked the idea of Houdini challenging anyone in the audience to manacle him.

Houdini hangs headlong (upside down) while escaping from a regulation strait jacket.

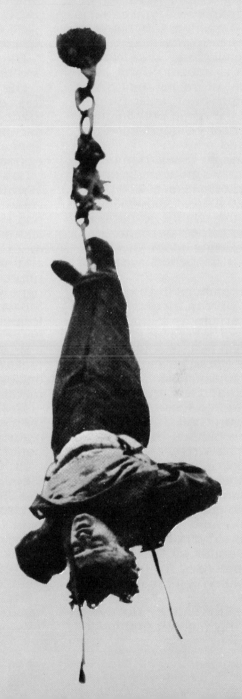

"Would you be prepared to be handcuffed by a police superintendent at Scotland Yard?" he asked the young American.

Houdini jumped at the suggestion. He went along to the Yard with the theatre manager and Scotland Yard detectives instructed him to put his arms round a pillar. They then handcuffed his wrists and prepared to leave the room.

"We'll come back when you've given up," they told him.

They had just reached the door when the handcuffs fell with a clatter on to the stone floor: Houdini had lived up to his reputation. He was free!

The Alhambra gave him an immediate booking and during his four week season he freed himself from every type of handcuff produced by members of his audience.

His London success resulted in demands for him to appear on the continent; within a year of leaving the USA he had become the top variety act in Europe. He was to make the name Houdini more famous than that of any other magical performer in the world.

Small, tough and, at times, bombastic, Houdini was not only a great magician and an expert on the mechanism of all types of locks, he was also a great showman.

He never lost the chance to publicise himself and he made the most flamboyant and extravagent claims about his skills – all of which, as it happened, were perfectly true!

During his appearances in Germany, a Cologne police officer named Werner Graff wrote an article in a local paper accusing Houdini of being a fraud. He said that Houdini's claim that he could escape from any type of official police handcuffs or leg irons was totally false.

Houdini demanded an apology and when Graff refused he took him to court for libel. In the court Graff challenged the American to free himself from a chain wrapped around his wrists and fastened with regulation police locks.

The chain and locks were the type used to control prisoners when they were being moved from one jail to another. As soon as Houdini found out the type of restraint that was to be put on his wrists, he secured a similar piece of prison equipment and practised for hours until he could be absolutely sure that he could make his escape.

The presiding judge ordered Houdini to be manacled in this manner and invited him to try to escape in full view of the court. This was something Houdini had never done before; all his stage escapes were behind screens so that no one could learn his methods.

However, once challenged, Houdini was not a man to back down. He agreed to attempt the escape but only in front of the judge and jury. Everyone else was ordered to leave the court room. Houdini was then chained by a prison officer and straightaway began to work himself free. First, he brought the chain upwards so that he could hold it in his teeth. Then he pulled and tugged until his left hand was free. Finally, he worked his right hand clear of the chain and was then able to swing the whole apparatus around his head with both hands. Houdini had again achieved the impossible!

The court fined Graff for his impudence and he had to make a public apology.

The German, however, appealed, and this time Houdini was shackled with a lock made specially for the occasion. He escaped in less than five minutes. Graff appealed again, to Germany's highest Appeal Court.

Houdini was headlining at the old Palace Theatre, Blackburn, when he received a cable from his German agent that Graff had lost the appeal: it was the third and last time. The German policeman had to meet all Houdini's costs, pay a large fine and had also to pay for the verdict to be printed as advertisements in all the Cologne newspapers.

It was in Germany that Houdini first performed the most sensational escape of his career: the Chinese Water Torture Cell.

He was lowered, head first, into a small tank which had been filled with water. His ankles protruded from the top, fixed in metal stocks.

The tank had a plate glass front so that his audience could see him clearly before a screen was placed around the contraption and he attempted his escape.

Outside the screen, two assistants stood with axes in case he failed.

It used to take Houdini two minutes to get free and appear wet, but smiling, from behind the screen. Sometimes he would remain hidden behind the screen and not show himself for up to twenty-five minutes – just to heighten the drama for the theatre audience!

I featured this great Houdini water escape in my last Christmas show on BBC TV – with my 18-year-old son Martin mak-

Martin Daniels hangs headlong, his feet in stocks, while rehearsing his escape from Houdini's water filled torture cell. He performed this feat on his father's Christmas magic show on BBC TV.

Paul Daniels, in the striped shirt, watches anxiously as Martin reaches the bottom of the glass fronted box. Note Martin's brother Paul standing by with a heavy metal sledge hammer to break the glass if things go wrong. A BBC man times Martin with his wrist watch.

ing the escape.

Previously, the BBC had sent a researcher to the Houdini Magical Hall of Fame in Niagara Falls where he was able to study the actual apparatus used by the famous American magician. This is owned by escape artist and collector Sidney Radner and is on loan to the museum.

Drawings and photographs were made and we also studied Houdini's instructions sent on in advance to the various theatres where he was to perform this particular death-defying feat.

One of his conditions was that the theatre had to provide 100 gallons of boiling water each night to ensure that, after the original preparations and 25 minutes stage explanations about the stunt, the water would still be warm enough for Houdini to enter.

The acutal Houdini apparatus was then copied here in England and built by my friend and magical associate Gil Leaney, one of the world's master illusion makers. There have been explanations in many books of how Houdini was able to perform this water illusion and it was featured by Tony Curtis in the role of Houdini in the Hollywood film version of his life.

But none of them used the exact method that Houdini used: Martin was the first.

The apparatus was completed just in time for the TV show at the BBC's Television Centre at Shepherd's Bush, London. In fact, Martin had only three days in which to learn how to do it and practise the performance. Rehearsals took place in a nearby garage.

Paul, my eldest son, came along to assist and two of us stood by with club hammers to smash the glass in case Martin couldn't escape in time.

At rehearsals, Martin had scraped his ankles badly and you may have noticed that when he appeared on television both ankles were bandaged.

There had been another hiccup at rehearsals: when BBC technicians tried out the apparatus without anyone inside they reported to me, "It's all right, Paul. You've nothing to worry about. We tried it ten times . . . it only failed once." Only once! That could mean Martin's life!

I insisted that even if the trick failed and we had to smash the plate glass to save Martin from drowning the BBC cameras should keep turning. In none of my TV shows is anything ever achieved by camera trickery; what you see on the screen is what actually happens in the studio.

Martin's actual escape was phenomenal. He was out of that tank in seconds and I will never forget the look of elation on his face when the screen lifted and he was seen standing on top of the tank itself. Martin's smile told it all. I was, indeed, a proud dad.

The speed with which Martin achieved his escape has astounded even professional magicians. One of them, in fact, claimed to have been specialising in escapology for twenty-five years and he refused to believe that anyone could break out of the Chinese Water Torture Cell in so short a time. He has challenged us to prove that it wasn't done by camera trickery.

The BBC would never lend themselves to fake such a stunt . . . and neither would I.

Martin holds his nose while hanging head downwards and preparing to escape. Beside the torture cell there is another heavy metal hammer . . . just in case.

Dangerous feats such as these ensured that Houdini remained a headline act until the end of his days. His death, in October 1926, came as a result of a university student punching him in the stomach in his dressing room at Montreal. The young man had asked the magician if he could sustain blows to his abdomen without injury. Houdini had only just said 'yes' when the youth punched him four times, without giving the magician time to brace himself.

Martin triumphant – wet but victorious on top of the cabinet after his escape. The bandages round his ankles are to protect them following injuries received at earlier rehearsals.

The blows caused internal bleeding and although Houdini insisted on performing that same evening and again the following night, he knew from the intense pain he was seriously ill.

From Montreal he went to Detroit. It was a Sunday night opening. He arrived late and, bathed in sweat with a temperature of 104, he went through the whole show. He was in agony. When the curtains closed he went back to his hotel where his wife called the doctor.

Houdini died on October 31st at the Grace Hospital, Detroit . . . the night of Hallowe'en.

This has now become America's National Day of Magic when magicians pay tribute to this great performer.

Houdini's life story has been filmed with Tony Curtis in the title role; presented as a stage musical; US magician Doug Henning has reproduced his Chinese Water Torture Cell in a live TV special on American TV and there have been numerous television documentaries on his career.

George Bernard Shaw, eminent critic and playwright, asked to name the three most famous people (real or imaginary) said 'Jesus Christ, Sherlock Holmes, Houdini'.

No magician could have a greater tribute.

* * *

It's all over . . . magician Paul leads the applause.

PARTY TRICKS

I've selected some party tricks for you in this section. Of course, any of them can also be performed as part of your own magic act but they are really more suited to being performed on their own as stunts for special occasions. Because of their similarity don't perform more than one of these at the same gathering.

The first of these special teasers is a mental test, involving the use of a book, in which the performer undertakes to find 'One Word in Thousands'.

Invite one of your audience to choose any number between 1 and 100. Get someone else to select a number between 1 and 25.

Hand your book to a third person and instruct them to turn to the page number which the first person selected. Then he must count down the lines to the number selected by the second person.

Tell him to put his finger on the first word of that line, to memorize it but not to identify it in any way.

Hand him a piece of paper and a pen and invite him to write down the word and fold the piece of paper. To ensure there is no peeping on your part announce that you will actually leave the room while this is being done.

On your return, take the folded piece of paper and hold it close to your forehead. Shut your eyes, pretend to be thinking deeply, and solemnly disclose the chosen word.

The explanation for this 'One Word in Thousands' effect is a very neat one:

you have a duplicate book in your pocket. You already know the page number and line before you leave the room so you quickly look up the word and reveal it when you return to your audience.

Select a small, slim paperback so it does not show in your pocket.

* * *

Here's a fine party telephone trick.

You will need a confederate you can trust and you'll need to make some arrangements beforehand. But, believe me, the simple preparation and rehearsal required will be well worth it.

Get someone at the party to spread out a full pack of cards with all the faces showing. Someone else must now place a coin on the face of any one of the cards. He has complete freedom of choice.

Without saying a word

you pick up the phone and dial a number.

"Hello," you say. "Is that the Wizard?"

You then hand the phone to your friend and the voice at the other end tells him the name of the chosen card. What could be more mysterious?

Here's how to pull off this particular miracle.

You actually tell your friend at the other end of the phone the identity of the card without any of your audience realising it. Suppose, for example, the chosen card was the four of clubs.

When you say the word 'Wizard' your friend on the phone starts counting aloud 'ace, two, three, four'; he must count slowly. When he says 'four' you speak again and say 'hello, is that the Wizard'?

This tells him the card chosen is a four. Your friend then says 'diamonds, clubs' and you immediately, before he names the other two suits, interrupt again by saying 'hold on a moment'. This tells him the selected card is a club.

Then hand the phone to

your friend and the voice at the other end of the line solemnly informs him "THE CARD YOU CHOSE WAS THE FOUR OF CLUBS"... and then immediately puts down the phone.

* * *

This is a subtle variation of the previous telephone trick which is well worth putting over at a party. I don't suggest you perform both tricks at the same party but if you are asked on another occasion and many of the same people are present you may well like to show them this alternative telephone mystery.

You need a number of articles on a table in front of you all borrowed from the audience. You can have as many items as you like but you must ensure that included are some keys, a watch, a 10p coin, a ball pen, a ring and a wallet.

Just before you start the trick, lay these articles in a straight line, remarking that you don't want to use too many articles and that half a dozen will be enough for your experiment.

Invite your audience to select any one of these items; then explain you met a very strange person a few days previously and this person possesses very strong telepathic powers.

He is so clever as a thought reader that if he is called up on the phone he will be able at once to identify the selected article, *without you, the performer, even speaking to him.*

One of those present then rings the number you give him and, without any hesitation, the voice at the other end names the selected article.

To achieve this astonishing effect you must use a small diary. Inside put down the following code:

KEYS	Mr. Black
WATCH	Mr. Green
10p	Mr. White
BALL PEN	Mr. Brown
RING	Mr. Blue
WALLET	Mr. Gray

You have this in your pocket. Your friend at the other end of the phone has the same code.

Take the diary from your pocket and pretend to look up the phone number of the thought reader. By this time, of course, you will know which article has been chosen and your book will tell you by which colour it is represented.

Give your assistant from the audience the telephone number, tell him to ring that number and ask for 'Mr. Black', 'Mr. Green' or whatever is the appropriate colour for the item chosen.

Your telepathic helpmate at the other end knows at once which article he has to name by looking at his own code, the duplicate of your own.

A colourful conclusion, eh?

* * *

If you have a friend who can play the piano you can pull off a musical mystery.

Ahead of time, prepare half a dozen cards with the titles of popular songs written on them, making sure that these songs can be played by your pianist assistant.

Invite your audience to secretly select a tune – the pianist can even be out of the room when the selection is made – then to take the appropriate card from those you have prepared and return it to you face down to ensure you cannot see the chosen song.

Ask the pianist if he can play the selected tune and, to everyone's amazement, he does just that!

To achieve all this, after writing out the songs on your cards (white ones are best, about 5×7″), secretly number each on the other side. Write the numbers close to the top left hand corner, as small as you can, so that when the cards are fanned out, face downwards, you are able to see the numbers at a glance. If you are handy with a paint brush you can paint a bright design or pattern on the back of your cards so as to

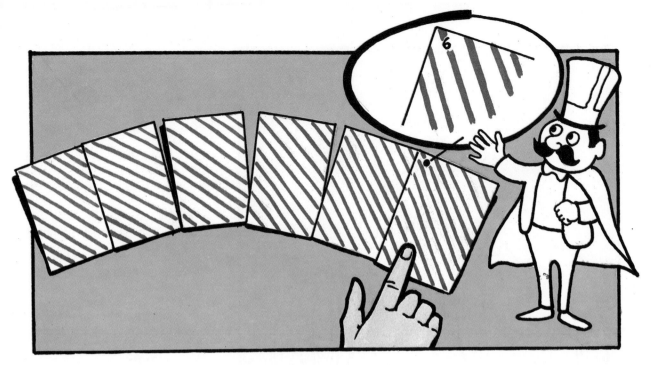

help hide the numbers.

Next, on a couple of small cards, write the numbers one to six with, alongside, the title of one of the songs. On the other side of these two small cards, which cover your secret code, write: 1 Ready; 2 Start; 3 Start playing; 4 All right, play; 5 All right, start playing; 6 Please start playing.

Once you know the tune selected you will have to secretly signal the title to the pianist. Your code will do this for you.

For example: if the third tune is chosen you say 'start playing'; if the sixth tune is chosen you say 'please start playing'.

The pianist can see from his own card which tune to play.

You'll have plenty of time to glance secretly at your card as the attention of the audience will be focused on the pianist. After some practice you should be able to memorize the code quite easily.

Alternatively, you could work out another code not entailing any speech, i.e., touch your left ear for 1; your left eyebrow for 2; your nose for 3; your right eyebrow for 4; your right ear for 5; your chin for six.

By signalling the *number* of the tune your pianist knows at once *which* tune to play. And you're both in business as magical musicians.

*　*　*

This party puzzler will produce gales of laughter if performed properly. Many professional magicians include it in their routine and it's unusual because the audience can see what is happening all the time, yet the victim is completely unaware of what is really going on.

Invite your assistant to sit in a chair while you stand to the left.

Have another assistant alongside you holding a box of tissues.

Take out several tissues and pretend to roll them in both hands so as to make a ball of paper about the size of your wrist.

Actually, you only roll the paper into the right hand.

Then separate your hands and draw your victim's attention to the left hand, which you keep closed – implying the rolled up paper is inside. Lower this hand to just below the chin of your seated assistant.

He or she will then be looking downwards at your left hand, when your right hand throws the rolled up ball of tissues over his head and behind the chair.

This is done on a level *above their line of vision* so they cannot see this happening. Open both hands and, of course, the ball of paper has gone.

Repeat this several times. The audience can see exactly what is happening but your victim will be completely in the dark.

I've seen assistants grab the performer's hands and look up his sleeves in their attempts to CHASE THE PAPER. And, all the time, the audience is laughing more and more at his mystification.

A proper paper chase, eh?

* * *

Removing a shirt from someone's back is always good for a laugh; it used to cause quite a sensation when performed by an old time American magician who went by the name of Jarrow.

He would select a man from the audience and then untie his tie, unbutton his cuffs.

Then, grabbing the shirt from behind, he removed the entire garment intact without disarranging his coat or waistcoat.

The explanation for stealing a shirt in this amusing manner is that the man who agrees to assist you is a stooge.

He has prepared his shirt in advance by putting it on like a cloak; the sleeves empty and his arms hanging down inside the unbuttoned shirt.

Only the collar is buttoned and the tie tied in the normal way. But the cuffs are buttoned around the wrists, leaving the sleeves free i.e., the stooge's *arms* are not in the shirt, only the *wrists*.

Any bulges will be covered up by the jacket.

Once the necktie is loosened or removed and

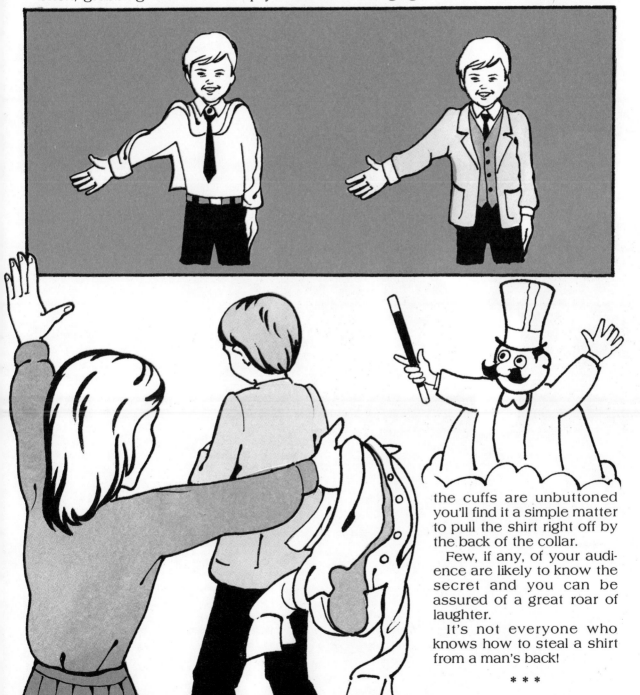

the cuffs are unbuttoned you'll find it a simple matter to pull the shirt right off by the back of the collar.

Few, if any, of your audience are likely to know the secret and you can be assured of a great roar of laughter.

It's not everyone who knows how to steal a shirt from a man's back!

* * *

Paul's magic hands.

Britain's two biggest magical societies are the Magic Circle and the British Ring No. 25 of the International Brotherhood of Magicians.

If you are over 18 you can join the Magic Circle as an associate member, but only if you are a male.

The International Brotherhood of Magicians is an American organisation with a branch in England and another in Ireland.

The IBM, as it is known, admits members of both sexes aged 16 upwards.

For details of Magic Circle membership write to the deputy secretary: Mac Wilson, MIMC, 29 Shepperton Road, Petts Wood, Kent.

British enquiries about IBM membership should be sent to the secretary: W.G. Strickland MBE, 'The Wand', Ferndown, Dorset.

Those of you living in Ireland should write to the secretary: A. J. Sharp, Irish Ring No. 25, International Brotherhood of Magicians, 43 Greentrees Road, Dublin 12, Ireland. If you live north of the border Mr. Sharp will put you in touch with his Belfast colleagues.

Don't forget to enclose a stamped addressed envelope with all your enquiries.

As well as these two main groups there are many more magical societies and clubs in London and the provinces. Many of them welcome both boy and girl members and this is not only a practical way of getting to know fellow magicians in your area but also to benefit from their advice and help.

Most societies publish regular newsletters and magazines filled with useful information about new tricks, ideas and presentations. They also have regular club meetings with practical demonstrations and lectures by experienced performers.

For those of you aged 15 upwards, I can also recommend a subscription to *Abracadabra*, the world's only magical weekly, which is published by Goodliffe Publications Ltd., Arden Forest Industrial Estate, Alcester, Warwickshire B49 6ER.

Magicians in this same age category will also find *The Magigram*, published monthly by The Supreme Magic Co., 64 High Street, Bideford, Devon, worth reading.

Write to either or both of these publications for subscription details.

Finally, for the budding magician, here's a list of British magical societies and clubs. I suggest you pick a club nearest to you and write for membership details.

They will be able to tell you at what age you can join and whether they admit both boy and girl members.

Again, don't forget that s.a.e.

A MAGIC CLUB

Aberdeen Magical Society
37 Carlton Place
Aberdeen AB2 4BR

Ace Magic Club
80 Wilshere Crescent
Walsworth
Hitchin, Herts.

Associated Wizards of the South
"Chevening" 48 Grange Road
Netley Abbey
North Southampton SO3 5FE

Magicians of Basingstoke
352 Abbey Road
Popley 4
Basingstoke
Hants RG24 9EJ

Barnsley Circle of Magicians
12 Burton Crescent
Monk Bretton
Barnsley
South Yorks S71 2QD

Bath Circle of Magicians
364 The Street
Holt
Trowbridge, Wilts.

Bexleyheath Society of Magicians
26 Brunswick Road
Bexleyheath, Kent

Blackpool Magicians Club
18 Conway Avenue
Normoss
Blackpool, Lancs.

Blyth Magic Circle
52 Barras Avenue West
Blyth, Northumberland

Border Magic Society
Summervale
Summergate Road
Annan
Dumfriesshire DG12 6SH

Bournemouth Society of Magicians
14 Campbell Road
Boscombe
Bournemouth BH1 4EP

Bradford Magic Circle
96a Heaton Road
Bradford, W. Yorks.

British Magical Society
125 Whitecrest
Great Barr
Birmingham B43 6EX

British Ring No. 25
International Brotherhood of
Magicians
"The Wand"
1 Dudsbury Crescent
Ferndown, Dorset

Burton Circle of Magicians
7 Twentylands
Rolleston-on-Dove
North Burton-on-Trent
Staffs.

Cambridge University Pentacle
Club
48 Holbrook Road
Cambridge

Cardiff Magical Society
9 Vicarage Hill
Newport
Gwent, Wales

Cavendish Knight of Magic
"Woodland View"
Preston New Road
Samlesbury
North Preston, Lancs.

Chester Guild of Magicians
29 Manor Drive
Great Boughton
Chester

Cleveland Magic Circle
227 Normanby Road
South-Bank
Middlesbrough
Cleveland

Cornish Magical Society
Red Lane Farm
Rosudgeon
Penzance, Cornwall

Cotswold Magic Society
41 Porchester Road
Hucclecote
Gloucester

Coventry Magic Circle
41 Avon Street
Upper Stoke
Coventry
West Midlands CV2 3GJ

Derby Magic Circle
114 Brookside Road
Breadsall
Derby DE7 6AH

Devon Magical Society
8 Hilly Gardens Road
St. Marychurch
Torquay
Devon TQ1 4QL

Doncaster Magic Circle
50 Coronach Way
Rosslington
Doncaster, South Yorks.

Dundee Magic Circle
Station House
Kingennie
Broughty Ferry DD5 3NZ
Scotland

East Kent Magical Society
14 Lovell Road
Rough Common
Canterbury, Kent

Edinburgh Magic Circle
6 Fleet Road
Tranent
East Lothian, Scotland

Exonian Magical Society
"Devonia"
28 Chesterfield Road
Laire
Plymouth, Devon

Fellowship of the Flying
Sorcerers
"Cornerway"
High Street
Claverley
North Wolverhampton

Fylde Mystics
70 Winton Avenue
Blackpool, Lancs.

Grand Order of Wizardry
167 Sickert Court
Marquess Road
Islington, London

Guild of Magicians
(Nottingham)
33 Greenacre
Edwalton, Notts.

Halifax Magic Circle
6 St. James Court
Halifax, Yorks.

Harrogate Society of Magicians
"High Winds"
38 Almsford
Harrogate, Yorks.

Hereford Magical Society
63 Widemarch Street
Hereford

Home Counties Magical Society
46 Rotherfield Way
Caversham
Reading RG4 8PL

Huddersfield Circle of Magicians
35 Butternab Road
Beaumont Park
Huddersfield, West Yorks.

Hull Magicians Circle
Westwood House
North Dalton
North Driffield
North Humberside

Ilford Magical Society
1 Moore Close
Norsey Farm Estate
Billericay, Essex

Ipswich Magical Society
27 Kirby Road
Walton-on-the-Naze
Essex

Irish Ring No. 25
International Brotherhood of
Magicians
43 Greenacres Road, Dublin 12
Ireland

Kilmarnock Magic Circle
5 Bowling Green Lane
Galston
Ayrshire, Scotland

Kirkaldy Magic Circle
84 Bridge House Hill Road
Bellfield
Kilmarnock
Ayrshire, Scotland

Leamington & Warwick Magic
Society
33 Price Road
Cubbington
Leamington Spa, Warwick

Leeds Magic Circle
5 Fawcett Road
Leeds, West Yorks.

Leeds Magical Society
31 Kirkwood Close
Cookridge
Leeds, West Yorks.

The Leicester Magic Circle
73a Kirkwood Road
Leicester

Lincoln Society of Magicians
33 Eastbrook Road
Lincoln LN6 7ER

Lincolnshire Magic Society
113 Hoylake Drive
Skegness
East Lindsey, Lincs.

Liverpool Mahatma Magic Circle
18 Wallgate Road
Liverpool
Lancashire L25 1PT

London Society of Magicians
6 Walden House
Pimlico Road
London SW1W 8LH

Luton Mystic Ring
21 Tarrant Drive
Harpenden, Herts.

Magic Circle
29 Shepperton Road
Petts Wood
Kent

Medway Magical Society
52 Elmfield
Gillingham
Kent ME8 6BN

Mercian Mystics (Cheshire)
5 Newlyn Avenue
Mossley
Congleton
Cheshire CW12 3AX

Middlesbrough Circle of
Magicians
6 Clifton Gardens
Eaglescliffe
Stoke-on-Tees
Cleveland TS16 9BB

Mid-Essex Magic Society
Oaklands Park
Tolleshurt
Knights
North Maldon, Essex

Modern Mystic League (Lancs.)
54 Poplar Street
Haslingden
Rossendale
Lancashire BB4 5LY

Mystic Severn (Dewsbury)
46 Caledonian Road
Savile Town
Dewsbury, West Yorks.

Newcastle Upon Tyne Magic
Circle
78 Kells Lane
Lowfell
Gateshead, Tyne & Wear

North Wales Magic Circle
165 Conway Road
Colwyn Bay, Clwyd

Northern Magic Circle (Lancs.)
Lazy Acres
The Croft
Back Lane
Grindledon
North Clitheroe
Lancashire BB7 5RW

Merlin Magical Society (Herts.)
24 Heath Drive
Potters Bar, Herts.

North West Society of
Magicians
25 Marylands Grove
Barrow-in-Furness
Cumbria

Northamptonshire Magic Club
5 Hartwell Close
Northampton, Northants.

Order of the Magi
2 Cedar Drive
Prestwich
Manchester, Lancs.

Oxford Magic Sphere
Merton College
Oxford

Paisley Magic Circle
13 Glebelands Way
Beith
Ayrshire, Scotland

Perth Magic Circle
22 Crammond Place
North Muirton
Perth, Scotland

Plymouth Magic Circle
20 Langley Crescent
Southway
Plymouth, Devon

Portsmouth Magic Circle
26 St. Peters Grove
Southsea
Hants.

Preston Magic Circle
193 Dunkirk Lane
Leyland
Preston
Lancashire PR5 35P

Scarborough Circle of
Magicians
26 Caymer Road
Eastfield
Scarborough, Yorks.

Scottish Conjurers Association
6 Crossburn Avenue
Milngavie
Lanarkshire, Scotland

Scottish Association of Magical
Societies
254 Nithsdale Road
Glasgow, Scotland

Scottish Magic Circle
"Racada"
57 Burn Street
Downfield
Dundee, Scotland

Sheffield Circle of Magicians
59 Hollythorpe Road
Sheffield, West Yorks.

The Society of Irish Magicians
43 Greentrees Road
Dublin 12

Southend Sorcerers Society
10 Cumberland Avenue
Southend-on-Sea

Staffordshire Magical Society
21 Southfield Road
Rotton Park
Birmingham, West Midlands

Sussex Magic Circle
64 Highdown Road
Lewes, East Sussex

Ulster Society of Magicians
26 Summerhill Park
Belfast BT5 7HE
Northern Ireland

Vectis Magic Circle & Allied Arts
18a High Street
Shanklin
Isle of Wight

Wessex Magical Association
12 Linden Road
Moordown
Bournemouth, Hants.

Wiltshire Associated Magicians
79 Trent Road
Greenmeadow
Swindon, Wilts.

Wolverhampton Circle of
Magicians
8 Bartic Avenue
High Acres
Kingswinford
Brierley Hill
West Midlands

Worcester Wizards
3 Gilmour Crescent
Claines
Worcester

York Society of Magicians
16 The Limes
Burniston
North Scarborough
North Yorkshire

Zodiac Magical Society
(London)
138 Village Way
Ashford
Middx.

LEARN YOUR TRICKS

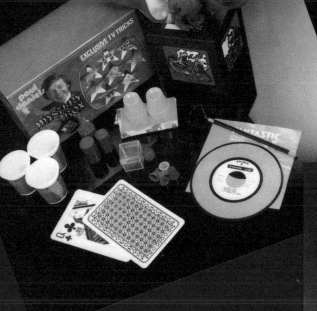

FROM THE MASTER

PUZZLE FUN

Match puzzles always have great appeal. But you must *only* work with used ones. For safety's sake, use pins or cocktail sticks. Place six matches as shown:

Then challenge your friends to add five more to make nine. Here's how to do it:

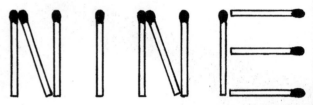

Show your audience five matchsticks and invite them to make them into two triangles. Here's how:

BEFORE

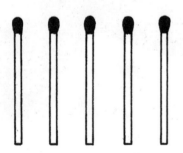

AFTER

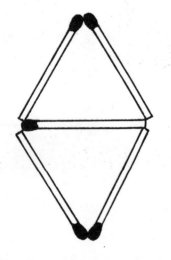

Place three matches as shown and ask someone to form an equal-sided triangle by moving just the one match marked 'B'.

BEFORE

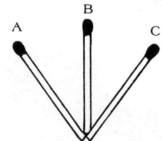

To achieve this, move the match 'B' as shown and the bases of the matches have then formed a very small equilateral triangle in the centre where the matches meet.

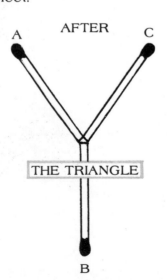

THE TRIANGLE

Put this question to a friend: 'What is half of twelve?' He's bound to answer 'Six.'

However, you can show him that half of twelve is seven.

To prove this, arrange eight matches to form a Roman twelve. Now, remove the bottom four matches and you are left with the Roman numeral seven.

You can vary this little puzzle by asking 'If I take four from twelve, what number would remain?' He's bound to answer 'Eight.' But, using the same principle you can prove him wrong. The remaining number will be seven.

BEFORE

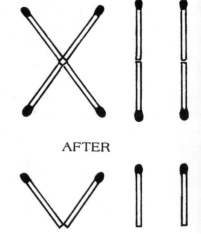

AFTER

Take three matches and challenge a friend to turn them into four. Like this:

Invite your friend to arrange three matches on the table so that they will make six. This is how:

Arrange 24 matchsticks as shown:

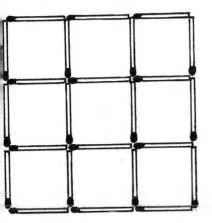

The puzzle is to take away eight of these and leave only two squares. Here's the solution:

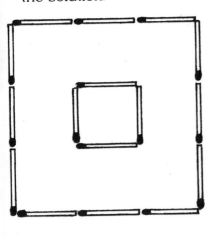

The problem this time is to turn nine matches into three dozen. No difficulty, really, if you do this:

Invite your audience to form five triangles with nine matches. Give them the matches and let them try and work it out. They mustn't break the matches. Here's how it's done:

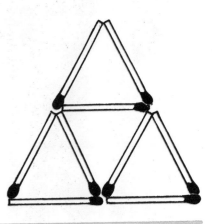

Arrange 17 matches to form six squares, as shown. The problem is to take five matches away and leave only three squares.

BEFORE

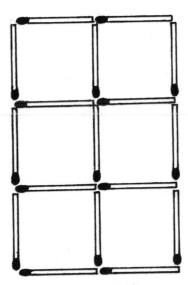

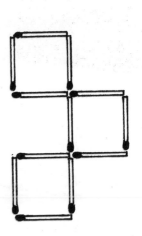

AFTER

This time arrange 17 matches in the same pattern and invite someone to take away six matches to leave only two squares. The solution:

DO-IT-YOURSELF TRICKS

Paul appears . . . from a previously empty box. A scene from his stage show at London's Prince of Wales Theatre.

DESIGN TO MAKE 3" SQUARE SHELL ALSO LARGER COVER

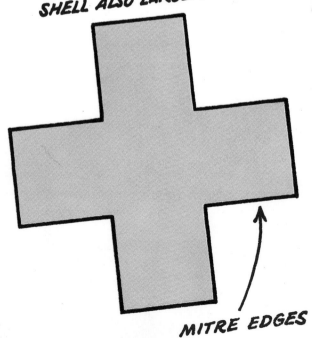

MITRE EDGES

I'm finishing my Magic Annual by telling you about some simple tricks that you can make for yourself on a do-it-yourself basis or get a handyman friend to make up for you.

The first effect is an up-dated version of an old classic – the vanishing die. Here the Victorian performer used to take a die (large dice) some three inches square and makes it pass through the crown of a hat.

Here's how you can modernise this old trick using a Rubik cube.

Rubik cubes can be bought for around £1 these days and you'll need two of them.

First make a shell cover to fit over one of these cubes. The cover, which should have one side open, can be in thin cardboard or tin, if you have a friend who is a metal worker.

An easy way to make this would be to place the original Rubik cube on your piece of cardboard and mark out, in the form of a cross, the size of the required shell; it has to be slightly larger than the original cube.

Cut this out, glue the corners (don't forget to leave one side open) and you'll finish up with a square shell which will fit easily over your Rubik cube. Cover the shell with black Contact or Fablon self-adhesives.

Now, with a sharp penknife carefully prise all the coloured panels from one of your two Rubik cubes and stick them on your shell to make it look like a scrambled cube.

You now have one genuine Rubik cube and one shell. Make sure the coloured squares are in the same position on each.

Finally, you will need to make a cover to fit over the fake cube; make it out of thin paste board which you can decorate with any bright colour to suit your fancy.

To perform, have the solid cube in one hand and the cover (fake cube hidden inside) in the other hand.

Place both on your table. Now borrow a hat or provide one yourself.

Pick up the genuine cube and tap it on the table to show that it is solid. Now place the cover and fake cube over it. On top of this place the hat, brim downwards.

You then invite the audience to watch very closely as you carefully lift the side of the hat facing you and remove the cover. Squeeze this slightly and the fake cube will remain inside the cover, leaving the genuine cube hidden beneath the hat.

Place the cover on top of the hat. Then remove it to show the fake cube inside. The audience will think this is the same one they saw previously.

Replace the cover and command the cube to fall through the hat. Now remove the cover again but this time you again squeeze the sides and the fake cube will again remain hidden inside.

Tilt the cover slightly, rattle the interior with your magic wand to prove that it is indeed empty.

Place the cover and its contents on one side, whip away the hat and there is the solid Rubik cube beneath the hat!

A real Rubik mystery!

* * *

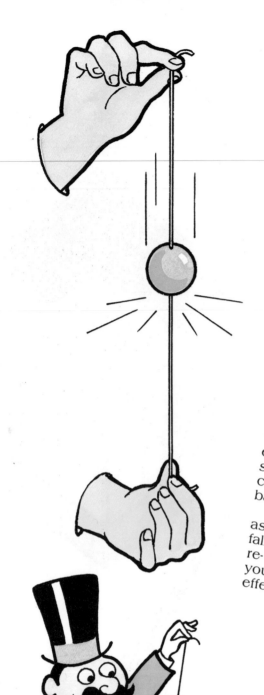

You can buy this next trick at any magic shop but you can also make it yourself.

At the start the magician shows everyone a small ball through which a length of cord has been threaded.

The cord is held at both ends with each hand but instead of dropping smoothly down the cord as expected, the performer is able to make the ball stop and re-start at will.

At the end of its downward flight he hands it to a spectator but he fails completely to control the ball's movements. Only the magician is successful.

The secret is in the ball itself. It needs to be solid, quite heavy and hard enough for a hole to be drilled through it. First, drill a hole straight through the centre. Next, drill a second hole leading off the first but rejoining it lower down. Both holes need to be wider than the cord used.

If you now thread the cord through the first hole the ball will drop from the top to the bottom of the string when you hold an end in each hand but if you thread the string through the second hole, which is curved, then you'll find you can control the ball's descent just by tightening the string.

This is how you perform the trick. Then, as if by accident, drop the ball so that it falls off the string. This will enable you to re-thread it before you hand it to one of your audience. You can achieve the same effect by using a small cube.

* * *

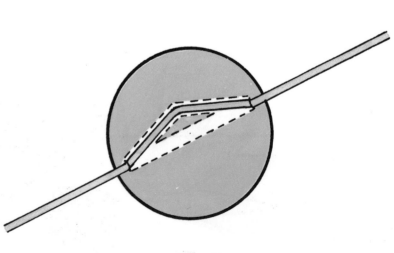

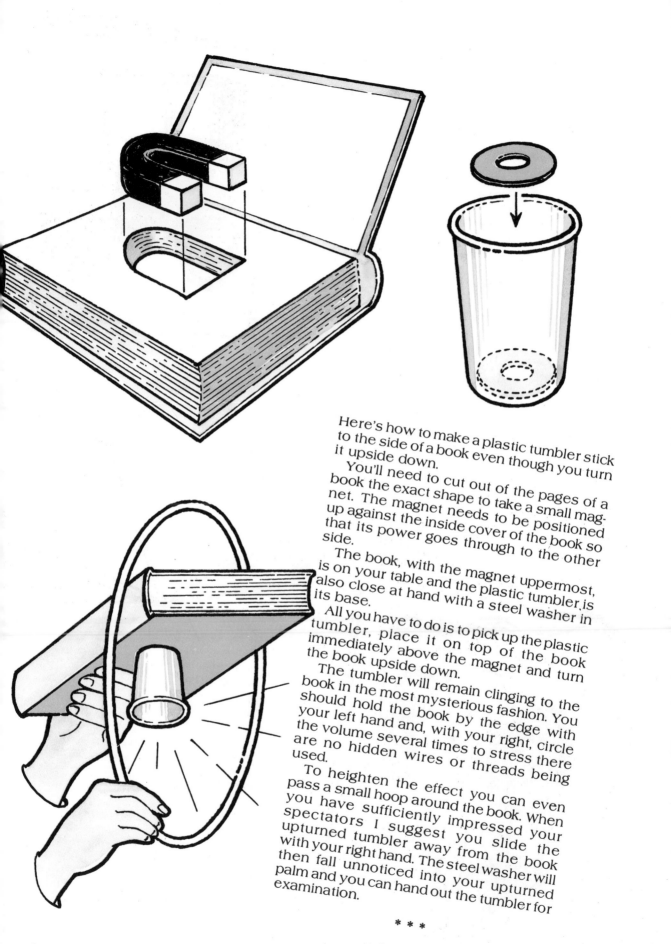

Here's how to make a plastic tumbler stick to the side of a book even though you turn it upside down.

You'll need to cut out of the pages of a book the exact shape to take a small magnet. The magnet needs to be positioned up against the inside cover of the book so that its power goes through to the other side.

The book, with the magnet uppermost, is on your table and the plastic tumbler is also close at hand with a steel washer in its base.

All you have to do is to pick up the plastic tumbler, place it on top of the book immediately above the magnet and turn the book upside down.

The tumbler will remain clinging to the book in the most mysterious fashion. You should hold the book by the edge with your left hand and, with your right, circle the volume several times to stress there are no hidden wires or threads being used.

To heighten the effect you can even pass a small hoop around the book. When you have sufficiently impressed your spectators I suggest you slide the upturned tumbler away from the book with your right hand. The steel washer will then fall unnoticed into your upturned palm and you can hand out the tumbler for examination.

* * *

For my final do-it-yourself trick I'm going to first give you the routine for its presentation and then the instructions for its preparation.

You must tell the story in your own words in your own style but here are the main points.

Tell you audience how you went into a stationers to buy a book on motor cars.

"The assistant said he had none in stock but just as I was leaving I noticed this book on the shelf with a picture of a motor car on its front cover. The assistant was unwilling to sell it to me because he said it wasn't really a book on cars; something had gone wrong in the printing and as a result it was all blank pages."

You then show your book is indeed nothing but blank pages.

"I asked why he kept the book and he said the strange thing was that every so often he looked through the book and he did find pictures of motor cars – like that."

And you show the blank pages are indeed covered with pictures of cars.

"I told him I thought this was very odd and he said it was even odder than I thought because sometimes he looked through the book and found no pictures of motor cars at all – instead, there were pictures of animals."

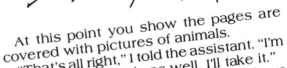

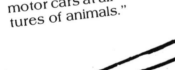

At this point you show the pages are covered with pictures of animals.

"That's all right," I told the assistant. "I'm very fond of animals as well. I'll take it."

"Well," said the assistant, "you can have the book if you like, but remember – it is a magic book and when you show it to anyone you may well find that it has gone back to blank pages again – as it has now."

You now show that all the pages are blank once more.

To prepare for this trick you need to buy a scrap book with thick paper, the thicker the better. You'll find one in a major chain store. First use the same illustration for the two covers – one the same side up as the following illustrated pages and the cover of the blank book upside down.

Turn over about six pages and paste in a picture of a motor car. Turn over a further six pages and do the same again. Carry on until you have filled every sixth page in this manner. Finally, paste a slip of paper at the top right hand edge on each page where there is a picture of a car.

Take the book again and paste on each page *before* the motor cars, pictures of animals. Continue until you have filled the book. This time paste a slip of paper at the bottom right hand edge of the pages on which you have pasted a picture of an animal.

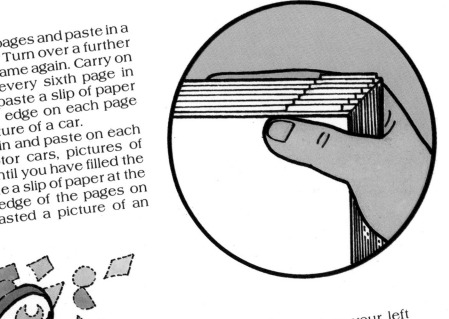

Now, if you hold the book in your left hand and flip through the pages with your right thumb at the top of the book, your audience will see picture of motor cars. If your thumb is at the bottom, they will see pictures of animals.

Finally, turn the book upside down, run through it a third time and you will see only blank pages.

This is a neat trick and well worth the preparation. If you are clever with a paint brush you can make your own pictures. The contrast then could be between flowers and birds or whatever interests you.

But don't forget that the back of each page must be left blank, otherwise you won't be able to show blank pages to everyone at the start and at the finish of your performance.

You have now come to the end of my Magic Annual for 1983. I hope you have enjoyed reading it just as much as I have enjoyed writing it for you.

Magic is a great art and a great hobby, whether you perform it or just read about it. But, either way, remember what I told you at the start - practise hard and never tell anyone our secrets.

Yours in Magic

Paul Daniels.